SECRETS
of Chaos and Mayhem.

Karmen Dalyte

ACKNOWLEDGEMENTS

To my mom Valda Riley, I miss you more than words can express. Losing you helped me to find me in the worst way. I was living and loving differently. After suffering the loss of you. My life changed. I'm no longer afraid of death. Because my all was taken from me to teach me how to live. The world cried the day you left. I rejoice in your spirit now.

De'Ann and Russell, my kids, I love you more each day. Thank You for your support in all I do. De'Yana my granddaughter, this is for you. Never be afraid to dream. You can make all of them come true. After all, you are the princess of the world.

Ida Bell, thank you for creating she that made me. R.I.P.

Queen Author Ms. Grad Marie (Gradneis Fontenot), thank you for helping me. There is not a day that goes by without a grateful heart for you. You have helped me when others would not. This is your craft, and you have welcomed me and helped me navigate. I did just as you told me. Just write. I'm still writing. Thank you for all your support and encouragement.

For the nonbelievers, thanks for the fuel.

CONTENTS

CHAPTER 1

DÉJÀ AND PETER

Damn! I hate being out here this late. My rent will be due in three days' time and I need three hundred dollars more to make it up. I often ask God why my life couldn't be like that of other young adults, that I watch going home to loving parents and free from worries. I can't tell you why my life is so different from other people, but I know from others that attend church that every person has a purpose or so they say, who knows; I guess I'm still searching for mine. I'm out here in the cold and on the streets at 4:15 A.M. This morning, why can't I get my hands warm? Look at this fool coming over here, Oh! Damn. (I know that's not a F.U.B.U. T-shirt.)

This dude smells like he hasn't had a bath in months, sheeeeeesh. I can already smell him from over here and he's still about twenty steps away from me. His eyes are big and bulging out of his head. His lips are as white as snow. Say you've got a dime? show me the money homes. I have the money, just give me the shit! Man show me the money or move around. Smack! Oh My God, I know this dude didn't just hit me and in my face at that. (And the chase begins). This dude must be high, everybody knows not to mess with Deja on this block, he's fast but I'm faster, I've been practicing with the track team of T.S.U. the local college in my hood. This dude has made it to the corner on me. I've got to be more careful. Bam! what was that sound? Ooh shit, he fell! I got that ass now. Who is that? Is that a dude standing over him or a girl?

This guy or girl is brown skinned with an athletic build. All I see are big waves and a ponytail of curls cascading down their back to the middle of their back, almond-shaped eyes that looks deadly. Green! No, hazel. What the Fuck! I know I'm tired but are my eyes playing tricks on me? Or, I'm I really tripping? A huge beautiful smile played on their lips that made me think there was music playing while I was watching him. This form is most definitely a dude. As I got closer, I noticed he's quite tall, maybe around six foot two. As I stopped running and walk cautiously to the scene unfolding in front of me, more of him is coming into view, he looks flawless. I find myself asking a question from an old school movie but in reverse; what's a guy like you doing in a place like this? Straight corny huh? Lol. A gangsta chick can be corny too. Men like that goofy hood type of chick. Hey, I'm only human. Oh my God, I hope I didn't speak those words out loud. He wore maybe a size eleven in shoes. Jordan's eleven cool greys no less.

He had very muscular legs as if he was a runner. I could see the cut of his muscles through the tight white T-shirt he wore. His arms looked very strong like he may have lifted weights daily. Veins looked like tree vines with tats covering them as far as you could see. He wasn't a big man, but he was the most gorgeous man Deja had ever seen. His teeth were very white against his creamy milk chocolate skin. Bright eyes not quite hazel or green but not dark brown either. Even his eyes looked like little chocolate pools sparkling. His eyebrows had a very faint arch, that looked as if they had been painted on or freshly waxed. His hair was very wavy at the top with the sides tapered and looked as if it would curl up into huge locks when wet. My heart was pounding so hard, could this be because I ran or because of his intimidating looks. I must have been staring because the beautiful man's eyes were slanted, and his face looked as if he was worried.

Are you okay? Are you okay? Then I felt a surge of electricity go through me causing me to jump badly. What? What did you shock me with? Huh? He pulled his hand back as if he had just been scolded. His face now had a strange look on it. We both jumped as we heard someone moving around on the ground in front of us. It was the guy that slapped me across my face, I immediately started kicking and punching him. He was struggling and trying to get me off him, that wasn't happening any time soon. I just heard Stop! The voice was so strong and forceful. I stopped in mid-air. I looked up to see the same guy that I was mesmerized by earlier. What? I shouted. He smiled and simply said "stop beautiful." He thinks I'm beautiful. Why is this very thin little girl trying to beat up this grown-ass man? She is really punching him and drawing blood from him. I must stop her; it seems as if she has zoned out, Cutie said. She's very nice with caramel colored skin. She has a set of large eyes that look like she has seen much more than her years should have allowed her to see. Her hair is pulled back in a ponytail with an H-town cap on. She has a round face with a set of pretty white teeth. Although she is small, she has a nice rack and ass on her.

I was watching her run and she had the grace of a sleek lioness running. Her lips are full, she has lip gloss on them making them look and shine like glass. The guy on the ground yells, get this crazy bitch off me! Before cutie could snatch me up, I punched the guy on the ground in the nose and face again several times. I got up. "Give me my shit back Yo!" I yelled. "Yo! shorty, why are you sweating old boy here?" Cutie asked. "Why are you in my business homie?" I got this! Ok. "Where's my shit? You better hand it over with your punk ass, NOW!" I pulled my nine-millimeter out from my waistband and put it to his head, "I WILL NOT ASK THE SAME QUESTION AGAIN." Oh my God! This dude just pissed on his self. "Look here shorty, get the gun out the dude's face." "Everybody has watched you chase this dude down and now you are going to kill him in the middle of the street? No shorty, don't do it like that." "Homie what's your name?"

The guy laying on the ground with chalk-white lips replied Henry. "Well, Henry do you have a family?" Yes. "Would you like to go home tonight in one piece?" Yes. "Alright then, Henry, please give this young lady whatever you took from her back now." His voice was trembling badly. "I would but I dropped it when she was chasing me." The handsome guy looked down at me and said: "do you believe him?" I replied "no, he's a feen that tried to jack me. He slapped me and ran away. This stupid motherfucker slapped me." The cute guy looked back down at the guy on the ground and asked, "Did you do that to her?" Henry is now afraid to answer. "Now, Henry, do you know who I am?" Henry replied, Yes. "So, you know exactly what I will do to you?" Yes, replied Henry once more. Cutie said, "I'm going to allow you to get up." I shouted; "I want my shit now!" cutie touched my hand and I immediately lowered my weapon. "Lil momma, let me handle this for you." "Look cutie, I don't need you to handle anything for me as a matter of fact," I stated and crossed my arms over my chest. Oh, man! did I just say that out loud? Dammit. I'm okay I got this. "Bae, see the problem is, I want to handle this for you because honestly." I know I wasn't tripping did he just call me bae. What the fuck? "Who does he think he is? Who is he anyway? He needs to be taught a lesson" the handsome dude said: "No man should ever hit a woman; I can't allow you to handle this.

I saw this guy running and I just had a feeling he had done something wrong, but, hitting a woman? That's straight criminal. So now Henry, how do you want to handle this? You owe the lady money plus you hit her. Now, what do you think would be fair to her but also teach you a lesson. I believe I need to remind you to never hit a woman." Henry started to cry...Please, Peter no! I will always remember, please no! Now, Henry you know I can't just let you walk away, what would people think? Henry is now crying uncontrollably. I don't know what people would think.

"Well, Henry let me tell you what they would think? They would think that Peter is soft and weak? Peter was stating to Henry. Although this is not my issue but since you have committed this street crime in my presence. I feel responsible for the outcome." Deja chimed in "Now, look here the both of you, since you feel the need to totally ignore me. Let me give you a brief insight into what I'm about to do. First of all, Henry is it? You're going to take a walk with me to the back of the store, and you are going to unass my money or suffer the consequences." Peter is trying to hold his laughter in. He knows she is serious, but he finds her very cute with this mean mug on her face. Not to mention the very funny feeling he had when he touched her.

Now she's threatening a man right in front of one of the deadliest dudes in Houston, TX third ward area. I turn to Peter, is it? I understand you want to help me, but I got this. Lil momma you already said that, but how am I supposed to let Henry make it and I'm involved now. Look, Peter, I don't know who you are, but I can handle my business. I've been doing this for a long time. Peter smiled again at me but this time the smile not quite reaching his eyes. Ok, Henry get moving. Henry is now in full-blown tears with snot coming down his face. I'm sorry, I'm sorry Peter, I didn't know that you knew her. Yes, I do know her, and she is a part of my family. I opened my mouth to say something, but the look on Peter's face silenced me immediately.

As the three of us walked to the back of the store. A very funny feeling is going on in my stomach. I've never killed anyone before, what if he kills him? Damn! Then he will have to kill me too because I'm a witness, shit. now I got my hands in my pockets, trying to think of a master plan to get out of this dilemma. Is a dime worth a feen's life? Damn, I didn't even know this dude's name was Henry until a few seconds ago. Peter has a look on his face that is so serious, and it looks as if he has a storm brewing within his soul. The look was frightening to say the least. Peter said, "Baby girl why don't you leave and let me handle this?" He reached into his pocket and gave me a handful of money. This should cover whatever he took from you.

CHAPTER 2

Peter said, "do you have anything to say to Lil mama." I looked at Henry and Peter with a smirk on my face. "My name is Deja." Peter repeated, "well, Henry, what do you have to say to Deja?" Henry spoke in a very low and strained voice, "Deja, I'm so sorry." I turned and walked away. As I left, I heard Peter ask Henry, "do you have any last request or words?" Henry said, "if you allow me to live, I will change my life. I promise you that. I will never hit a woman again. Smoke or take anything from anyone ever again." Peter contemplated on the statement. Henry started crying and speaking again. "Peter, I know who you are, and I will never cross you or her again I swear." Henry remembered Peter from being a very small boy early in his years before crack cocaine hit the streets. He was a principal at a Middle school. Peter Paradise Pho was a gifted child, any skill he was taught he adapted to quickly and excelled in it. He spoke several different languages and even wrote poetry as well as played many instruments in the school band. One day he was at the school in the after-school program and three much larger boys from the local high school Yates, cornered him and beat him badly. I witnessed it and ran them off. I called the police and ambulance to take him to the hospital. I checked on him several times, and one day he just vanished into thin air from the hospital after several months of physical therapy, never to be heard from or seen again.

I remembered him only because of the blackbird's tattoo that was on his left shoulder blade that continued to his neck. He told me one day after practice many years ago that he had tattooed the blackbirds because he had read that blackbirds have an extraordinary meaning. They symbolize knowledge and they are the carriers of intelligence and quick wit. So, everyone born under this totem or everyone with a blackbird, as a spiritual animal has a great tendency of being extremely filled with understanding and intelligence. Even then a child was schooling me, a college educated man, just like today again I was his student. I asked him, "you don't remember me?" He looked at me closely and said, "no, why should I?" In a faint voice, Henry added, because I saved your life. Peter looked closely to realize this was his old principal. Mr. Jones. Henry Jones.

CHAPTER 3

I woke up the next morning in an unfamiliar place, I looked around and then realized that I got a room in the local Hilton hotel where ballers stayed in the Galleria area, then I became at rest. As I sat up in bed, the memories of the night before ran through my mind. Man, what a night. After all that drama, I called a cab at the next corner from my cell phone and found myself a room to lay low and try to figure out a plan. I didn't know what he had done to the guy, but his look was disturbing when I left them. I turned the T.V. on to the local news channel 10. After watching for a minute, I laid back in bed. Oh my God, I couldn't stop thinking about his touch, it was like a lightning bolt that shot straight down to my vay jay jay, making me wet. We are in a new BMW; the seats were so soft.

I look down and see the nice black leather seats, the seat warmer must be turned on because, my ass is super warm…it's snowing now, and we are parked by a lake or a river. I look to my left and his chest is going up and down very fast and his breathing is heavy. He has a smile on his face, but his eyes are closed. We were driving and I looked over and told him I want you now, he opened his eyes and looked at me for a second and winked. Our code for telling me to pull over. My baby has always given me whatever I wanted since our chance meeting, so, I must be very careful with what I ask him for, because he makes the impossible possible when it comes to me.

As we pulled over to the side of the road. I leaped across the console into his lap. As our lips touched, the kiss deepened, our tongues were in a dual all on their own, each time he kissed me was like the first time. His lips were always soft, and he always tasted of mint. He loved chewing gum. I always made him lick my gum, because it seemed to make it sweeter. That tongue was velvety soft. I loved to kiss him. I kissed him open mouthed, and then slid my tongue down, to the side of his neck which was his hot spot. I traced my tongue down to the left side of his neck where my name was tattooed, this turned him on. I continued to turn him on, by licking and touching him everywhere my tongue would reach and burn a hot trail. I moved to his nipples after destroying the very expensive shirt he wore. I licked and sucked each one. His seat was pushed all the way to the back seat allowing us more room.

As I unbuttoned his jeans, I was thinking hello sunshine. His erection was hard as always, standing at attention, like a very tight tent in his Sean John boxers. His inches and girth were intoxicating just to see it. I wasted no time deep throating him. My mouth was so wet and warm, he was moaning, as I was licking slowly at first, and then faster and faster, going deeper and deeper. He was so deep in my throat I was gagging and moaning those alphabets. He was holding my head and pushing himself deeper inside my throat. I loved the pain and pleasure all at once. We were both moaning. He was telling me, bae, I'm about to cum.

As he started massaging my scalp, I knew he was about to erupt in my throat. Baby hold on a minute, I raised up, just as I got over him, he rammed his very handsomely large penis into me, driving me to sheer ecstasy. I could only grab the seat and hold on for my most wonderful ride. He was entering me hard and fast. I did the move he loved, I reversed cowgirl on that dick. Now I'm facing him and kissing those very succulent lips.

I was about to reach that Green Giant climax he had brought me to. Sucking my small mountains of nipples. I was now almost howling from his lips alone sucking my peaks. Rotating my hips, a climax at bay...knock knock! Bam bam, damn it! What the hell is that? It's the fucking door. I grabbed my Nina and hand on the door. Fuck, did I pee on myself. I ran to the door. I'm so pissed off and pissed on or wet. I just snatch the door open. My mouth fell open; what the fuck! Why are you at my house? I mean in my room. At my room? Dammit. My confused ass. Did I dream this dude up? My hair is all tossed up. I don't even have any lip gloss on my damn dry ass lips. He must be saying, "damn, this chick always looks whack as hell." I hadn't even gotten out of the bed yet today.

Luckily, I paid in advance for four days for my room, as well as paid my rent last night with the money he gave me. I just needed a clean place to get my mind straight. There's that small grin again as though there's a comedy show going on in his devilish, sexy, handsome, ass head. Oh God, does he know what I was just doing? I don't even know what I was doing. No, he couldn't, I was dreaming. What if I was moaning loudly? What if I called out his name? What is his name? I'm Peter or P3 on cue, his sexy ass said like he read my mind. Shit? We just stared at each other for what seems to be years going by. Peter was the first to speak up; Lil Momma, how's it going? I replied, what's up Gangsta? We both smiled. You didn't answer my question? Humm. Did he just lick his lips? Damn, that was sexy. L.L. lips didn't have anything on his. It seemed like time stood still for a moment. What question was that? Why are you here? Oh, yea Lil momma, I just wanted to check on you. As you can see, I'm fine.

He licked his lips again and I became frustrated. Why was L.L. Cool J's song, "I need love" playing in my head? Why did this frustrate me so much? Was it because I wanted to kiss him so badly? Or, could it have been that damn dream that woke me up wet in all the wrong places?   I've never experienced something like that before. I have never dreamed of a man much less fantasized about one before. What! I snapped again. Wait a minute Lil momma, what's wrong? Just as I was about to answer him. He pushed the door open and dashed into the room. What is that in his hand? Why did he have a gun? His eyes are slanted again like he's straining to hear something. Peter, Peter… I repeated, there is no one in the room. He then placed his gun in the shoulder holster and smiled, Lil pretty, you're going to make me dead something? Okay, Lil pretty. You looked very fluttered and then you seem to have this attitude, like I was disturbing you, or like you had company?

No, I was just chilling, I had a nightmare, or a disturbing dream. Is that why you are soaking wet in certain places? He looked down and I was wet as if I had pissed in my pants. I was so embarrassed. Hey, will you excuse me for a moment. I walked in a rush to the restroom, I meant to close the door but left a crack in the door by accident. As I stripped down to my birthday suit, I got under the hot spray of water, shampooing my hair with my favored scent of coconut shampoo, I lathered up my luffa and washed my body slowly. Peter tried to turn his head but couldn't stop himself from watching her, she was beautiful, and he wondered if she knew how beautiful she was. Just the way she was, he wanted to be around her. He silently promised to get to know her. He would be around to see this beautiful flower bloom. He wanted to be the one to nurture her and water her to help her grow.

As I showered, the water felt so good, it had been a long time since I was able to shower using both hot and cold water. I had a nice little apartment on the southside, fully furnished with items from the local Goodwill's or Savage shops. My place reflected my taste in shades of pastels, stripes and colorful arrays of silks and linen. Peter reflected to Deja in the shower, he now heard music playing. Was that always playing in the background? Tupac's "I Ain't Mad at You?" After his little peep show, he wasn't mad at her at all. He could see she was rapping every word of the song. Next, "Draped Up" by Bun B and Lil Keke came on and she rapped that like a member.

This Lil Lady was intriguing, looking like a beauty queen and rapping like a street thug. She was getting out of the shower, so he once again tried to turn his head. As she came out of the shower, the thick mist clouds of smoke started to clear, they locked eyes. Were her nipples hard? Did he just smile at me? She lowered her gaze and went to close the door. He was happy she did because for some reason he was walking towards the restroom. The trans was broken.

He looked around the nice room and thought to himself; she has nice taste. He wanted to know more about her. Meanwhile, I was in the restroom wondering how his eye color changed so much and trying to catch my breath. I had left my clothes in the other room where the devil was. I couldn't think of a better way to describe him besides that. When I walked back into the room, he was still there, taking up the whole room with his overpowering presence. I walked over to my backpack then realized I had not packed any clothes. Peter thought her perplexed look was cute to him. He would have to teach her to master her poker face. When I went back into the restroom and put on the clothes from last night. He said, let's go grab a burger, Lil pretty. I looked at him crazy then my stomach rumbled.

We both laughed and then I said ok Gangsta. As we walked down the hall to the elevator, there were eyes on them. Peter sensed it and remembered to make a note. He put his hand on the small of my back and electricity shot through us simultaneously. He moved his hand but remained closed to my side. As we left the luxury establishment, he guided me to the parking lot, there was his black beamer waiting, this brought back memories of my dream, I almost needed another shower at this point. I looked down at the license plate that read, P3. I made a mental note to remember it.

As we whizzed through the streets, I took notes of my surroundings, this was a nice area not far from the hotel. We arrived at one of the best steak houses in Houston. As soon as we reached the door the maître D opened the door. Hello, Mr. Pho, oh! He's got clout in these streets! Ok. We followed him to an upstairs area that the building didn't look like it had. As we were getting seated, the maître D asked him, did he want the same menu as usual? Peter said let's let the lady order. I looked over the menu and let out a small gasp as I saw the prices and my eyes met his. Peter said, "order whatever you would like," I don't have any food allergies, so guess at my order. He let out a smirk wondering what I would order for him. I asked for the special menu that I had only read about in magazines.

I knew wealthy people only ordered from that menu. The waiter gave it to me. It was called the blacklist, fitting for the place we were at. I quickly scanned the menu and ordered roasted sea bass with asparagus, baby carrots with pilaf quinoa. For my drink I ordered Dom and I ordered him a double shot of Remy. Peter smiled because this would have been the exact order, he always ordered for himself. I was smiling because my thoughts were, if he got it, spend it. Let him know you've got taste but not the money yet, either he respects it or move around.

CHAPTER 4

There was a funny feeling in my stomach. I never ignored that feeling since I was a kid, Peter was very in tune with himself. That one time I did, was the day my life changed forever. My eyes were alert as I watched the cars on the ground move briskfully. I also paid close attention to the two large buildings in the area. I knew this area well. I even had one of many properties in this area in which I resided. As we finished up lunch, we moved to another secret area in the restaurant where a pool table was. There were several other men in the area smoking cigars and drinking expensive Scotch or Cognac. I felt out of place in my Fila tennis shoes and a t-shirt with jeans. But I carried myself like an heiress though. Head held high and back arched over the pool table causing Peter's mind to wonder, How the hell does she keep doing this to me. I'm usually so focused.

I can't stop myself from wondering what she tastes like or wanting to see her naked again. We looked at each other and the time always seemed to stand still as she exhaled, and I inhaled, it was like she was breathing, and I was inhaling all of her. We started looking at other people and she started to mouth what she thought they were saying. It was cracking me up, I even joined in. We were on a roll. It was like we had known each other forever. Our flow was effortless and smooth. As we made our way out of the restaurant, that sick feeling got super strong. My car was sitting curve side, I tipped the maître D as he opened Deja's door. My phone was on speed dial to the F.B.I. if the need arose.

The F.B.I. stood for Felons by Initiation. My longtime friends, that if called upon came through and nothing was left breathing. My crew was made up of my two friends. We found our way to each other through a lot of death and chaos. Michael (Mike) Porter and Deleon (Death)Vegas. As my car left the curve, I noticed a guy that was at the bar walked out of the restaurant after us. He got into a silver 2 door Jaguar. As we got to the light. I noticed the same car pull up next to us. The dark-skinned guy was on his phone, but the strange part was he was fluent in Spanish and because I also understood Spanish, I heard him say "No se preocupe, ambos son muertos caminando." No worries they're both dead people walking. I continued to listen to Many Men by Fifty Cent playing from my Bose system. I then reached into my middle console, where my double barrel 1911 pistol with quad wield rapid fire was, it shoots 20 rounds in 1.5 seconds rested. Both of my Italian made guns were customized, with P3 inscribed on the handle. I turned to Deja she also was very keen on what was underway. She winked at me, and then showed me her baby 9mm with 50 round clips. I was like, damn, baby girl got it going on. Deja was jamming out and bouncing in the seat all along checking and loading her gun. I told her to pat her feet to the beat, just as she did, she noticed the floorboard shifted and exposed a small arsenal of weapons in my ride. I told her to lay her seat back and relax. Just as she did that, two grey Range Rovers matching the same paint as the Jag were placed strategically on either side of us. I told her to reach down and zip the seat covers over her upper chest; the material was made from a fabric created by me to be bulletproofed with a Teflon base. She was so petite it looked like a snuggle surrounding her. Just like soldiers in action, the bullets started to fly.

My car was bulletproofed as well, but just the thought of Deja getting hurt, made the beast in me come out. I'm on ready, and my beamer was sitting on run-flats. I looked in my rearview mirror and noticed one of the range rovers hanging back, then the noise started. Shots rang out. Big mistake, a huge mistake. As I turned to Deja she was laughing and firing off rounds, just then, as I got to the corner and instead of going right, I shot across two lanes and went left. Shooting into the windshield of the range rover that chose to lag behind, killing the driver because the truck started flying across the other lanes. As the truck slammed full force into a car parked on the street, I saw the bodies of two men sprayed all over the street. Just as one of the bodies landed, he was run over by a speeding fire truck, blood was everywhere.

Deja looked back and for a brief minute, I thought I saw a look of fear, but just as soon as it came it was gone. The other range rover was closely behind us, but that's only because I allowed it to be.

As I played with them, my homies Mike and Death weren't far behind us. Once the floorboards were activated, it also sent out a signal notifying my boys, that I needed help. We all had this F.B.I. gangster signal in our rides. They looked like a luxury ride but were packed with death. We all had designed various secret compartments in our homes and cars for war.

As I played cat and mouse with them waiting on Death to come through, we were now approaching traffic. Just as we reached the intersection and the light turned green. Death's toy Jeep appeared, and the back of the hatchback opened, as I heard a train coming through one of his signature murder songs by Jigga Train by Foxx, I slowed down almost to a complete stop, as I turned my car sideways, so that all the cars in the traffic were shielded behind my car on the single-lane street. The sound of war erupted on the Houston downtown streets, as Death Tommy gun sprayed the range rover. The truck flipped and landed inside an abandoned building. Then a black van with several men were gaining on us, just then, a muscle car came burrowing down the street, It did a donut and the driver of that car started shooting causing the van to flip. The driver jumped out and ran to the van and snatched out one man who must have been dead because he threw him to the ground. He then disappeared to the other side of the van. We sped up to match speed as we flew throughout the back streets, I noticed the grey mustang following us just as Deja was reaching down to pick up yet another gun, I told her he's with us. She smirked and turned Up "Bust It Baby" by Plies on the radio. As we sped down the street jumping on the freeway. When we hit the Sugarland exit, a suburb of Houston. Some miles later, Deja relaxed as she saw both of my friends following us. As we pulled into the beautiful area Deja was in awe.

We went deeper into an area secluded that looked like a scene out of an island paradise. Water was everywhere and huge trees made a line with colorful flowers along the side of the driveway. The house looked more like an office building. With multiple garage doors. As we each used their garage door openers, the doors opened to reveal all kinds of equipment. As we all exited the cars, the garage door closed and a gate made out of some kind of chain link closed, as well as from the inside. It was so weird I had witnessed some very strange gadgets today. It had me wondering just whom Peter or P3 was? As they started giving secret handshakes and watching me curiously.

I stood by the car. As Peter eyed me, he started to smile and said meet Mrs. Pho, the guys looked from us both, and then started to greet me with hugs. Just then I heard a loud cry and looked at the trunk of the mustang. Mike walked over and opened it to a man jumping out swinging wildly. Just as fast, the guy Peter had called Death, hit him with a two-piece combo. Those punches stopped all the childlike swinging. The man fell to the floor painted like a marble sky. This was one of the guys from the van, Mike had rescued or captured him from the accident after being identified as one of the shooters shooting at us.

CHAPTER 5

Once the man woke up, he had been drugged enough not to sleep but to feel all the pain they administered. His eyes felt very dry as he looked at the mirror placed in front of him. He realized both eyelids were missing and saw them placed on a tray next to him. He tried to cry out, but for some reason, no sound came out. He also saw something that was large that resembled kneecaps. Mike added another drug in the I.V. that was in his chest. Now he could speak. The crew was standing around waiting. As he tried to scream, I hit him in the temple with the butt of my gun. When he regained consciousness after the next drug was given, he was told to start talking. The Who? What? Why's? And When questions were asked, he was told to cooperate more, and every time he resisted, a limb or body part was removed.

I couldn't watch anymore, so I went into the house and started making dinner. I cooked like a five-star chef from watching the food network all the time. As a hobby in between hustling, the kitchen was my playground. Peter had just finished removing the man's vocal box through his nose and dipping him inside acid like a chocolate fondue. When Peter entered the beautiful kitchen that had every gadget known to man and some not, due to Peter's creations. I could see now both myself and Peter were very twisted. As a child, I was adopted by a couple that owned a meat market. I had seen all kinds of animals killed and taxidermy, but I had never killed anything personal until today. Peter was the son of a billionaire and the head of the Triads. The Triads is a traditional criminal organization that operates out of South Asia but are worldwide.

His mother was an engineer that loved to create. Peter's mother and father were killed in a violent array of bullets when the triads crept into his family's mansion to overthrow his father's power. After he wanted to move to the states and raise his family. With too many secrets known by his father, the order of death for the family was handed down. His mother had created several weapons that she and his father had used to try fighting back, but the house not being a fortress to protect them, their fight was in vain. Although his mom Ida Bell had created a safe room, which saved his life on that faithful night. His parents couldn't be spared. He would always hate that. That was the start of his creations, the smart house he created, was more protected than the Pentagon. He even owned the air above his property, so nothing could fly too close over it or in the area. His forty miles of property was like a Brinks safe.

CHAPTER 6

Deja felt at home in the beautiful home, no, mansion. I hadn't been in an office building that was this big or beautiful. As I cooked, I listened to music. "So, What" by Ciara came on my YouTube station as I diced vegetables. I was in my zone. I had clicked out. I was wondering where I had seen the guy from the garage at. I just could not place it. The crew had killed him before I could question him alone. I came out of my daydream and Peter was tuned in on me. As I hummed along with the music, Peter memories faded back to being a kid. Running around his family home. His mom and dad were very important people, but they always had time for him. Plus, he had a host of Aunts and Uncles. Well, he thought them to be family, but most were trained killers. Hired by his parents to protect them at all costs. Each one had lost their lives on that night many years ago.

His parents had just thrown a private pool party for the family when it seemed like the shadows had come alive and left a river of blood around his family home. The crystal blue water, that had just been so refreshing and breathtaking was a deep red crimson color, with body parts floating as far as the eye could see. Once the screams began his father and mother took him into their bedroom, where there was a hidden room. It was concealed behind the chandelier that even the staff never knew about. It was a very beautiful room, with 3 queen size beds and a refrigerator, a portable stove, even vents for the smell to disappear before the scent hit the air. There were all his favorite toys and board games. Multiple flatscreen T. Vs, two full restrooms and enough food to last exactly two months. He had known because he had resided in that beautiful space for just that long, until the Triads couldn't find him and they returned after the death of his parents and he had not been seen, and no bodies were found.

No one had given his parents a funeral. Since the order had been to kill all heirs of Peter Pho Sr or P2 his father. The death warrant was still in effect even after all these years. That beautiful room had become a cell. The night the Triads returned, he left the protection of his hiding space and went to his mother and father's room. He would often go there when he missed them to find something with their scent, to take back to his space with him. After his parents kissed him that night, they all must have known it was their last goodbye, because they hung onto one another, sharing loving embrace's and thousands of kisses, are just holding each other's face and trying to memorize each feature.

His mother was so beautiful, with locks that hung down her back, that looked as if they were strong enough to pull a car. She had large round eyes that danced to the sun and moon, hazel that changed to green with flakes of gold in them. Her skin was the color of a new penny, that shined like it had been kissed by the gods themselves. Her lips were always velvety smooth.

She would always read to him and show him how to design toys he wanted on T.V. By the time he was 7years old, most of his toys had been built by him and his mom. She would say, as long as the structure is strong you can build from there. His mother was tall, to Peter anyway. She seemed to be as tall as the Statue of Liberty, but she wasn't because that would mean his father was King Kong's height. Peter smiled just thinking about his parents As a kid, everyone was so big. Ida Bell was a slim southern woman, that loved art. That's how she and his father met. She was running down the street in New York, on her way to an art show, when she bumped into a very handsome businessman, getting out of his luxury car. It was raining and she ran right into him.

Once he set his foot on the curve, she fell, and he picked her up out of the rain. He then took her to lunch after buying her a new dress, for the art show that she missed. He later paid for a private showing for her. His father was 6 ft 2. He had curly hair, cut very low to the sides of his head. He had emerald green eyes, that look like gems when he smiled and that would turn dark when worried or troubled. A small nose that he would twitch to make his son laugh as a small child, and a smile that would cause a woman to pause. He had the looks of a GQ model but was inked up under his clothes and very skilled at deadly combat. As a child, he would sit for hours and watch his father practice fighting. Using weapons made by Peter's mom.

After Peter heard noises in his home after months of silence. He ran to the phone, that sat on the table next to the bed in his parents' room, which hid the button to the elevator that hung over the bed. He jumped in just as he saw men checking doors in his home. Looking under the beds and throwing his parent's items all over the beautiful home. He noticed one of the men giving out orders, and he was a friend of his father's. He thought the man to be dead. Just as the men entered the master bedroom, he dashed to the air condition vents, where he had stored guns from his parents, cash and clothing, and a cell phone. The two months in the hidden space, he had learned several different languages fluently. He had also perfected the skills of fighting like his father. He would kick and punch for hours until his little arms and legs were red and sore, the bruises healed, and he knew he could excel but he never stopped until the punches or kicks were perfect.

As he navigated through the air vent ducts. He was able to hear and watch the men. When the orders were given to burn down his family home, he lost it. The memories of his mother and father flashed through his head, as he moved almost silently through the vents. He got to the library of his home and went into his family secret safe. His parents had always told him to protect that in which you love. Your history is here at your fingertips. He removed items along with several papers, also pictures, he stuffed them in his bag. As he approached the door, he heard voices. So, he looked around for something to protect himself with. His father's gold letter opener was on the desk. He retrieved it. He gripped it tightly as he ran as fast as he could towards the double doors. When they opened, he stabbed the man he remembered in the left eye and pulled the letter opener halfway through his face, with so much force that Peter heard the skin tearing like a harsh paper.

The man fumbled to get the gun he had dropped when Peter launched at him. Just as they both were reaching for the gun. Another man ran in and Peter shot him in the throat and chest. He grabbed the first man causing both of them to fall and Peter continued to hold the trigger hitting them several more times. Peter had so much blood on him it looked as if he had been dipped in red paint. He made his way to the forest that surrounded his family home and that's where he remained for weeks scared to leave. Uhmmm excuse me? Earth to Peter. Hello? P3? I don't know what to call you. As she got closer to touch him his hand went out to stop her. Hey, are you okay? Deja asked, Peter smiled and said yeah, I'm sorry, I flashed out for a minute you know. I laughed and said yeah, I guess killing does that to you. Just then Mike and Death walked into the kitchen. The smell of food brought them right to the stove. I told both killers, don't you dare touch my pots. Peter laughed and shrugged his shoulders as he said you heard her. The two men looked as confused as small children getting chastised by their mothers. Even though both men had used beyond professional cleaning supplies to clean up and wash their hands, they rushed to the kitchen sink and washed them again in front of me. As they all helped to take the feast, I had prepared to the dining room, which had been decorated with fine china and crystal wine glasses.

Peter stood back, taking it all in before he walked over and kissed me passionately, causing Death and Mike's mouth to drop open. Although Peter was handsome and single, In his 22 years and 9years of knowing them, they had never witnessed such an exchange between him and a woman of his liking.

CHAPTER 7

While we all sat and stuffed our bellies full of fried chicken, candied yams, smothered cabbage, red beans, and rice, creole mac and cheese, green beans with bacon and potatoes, honey buttered cornbread. You would never have guessed that they had just made a whole person disappear, and rained chaos down on the Houston streets, just hours ago. With the garage cleaned and sanitized, looking like a new add on to the home.

No one would have ever known the body count of lives taken there. After dinner, the men cleaned up to allow me some time alone to process my environment. As they drank beers and wine cleaning the kitchen, they asked Peter about Deja. So, P, where did you get that fine specimen from? Death asked. Both Death and Mike kept throwing questions and when he turned around to them and said I rescued her yesterday in an alley, they both burst out in laughter and said this guy here be straight tripping.

Peter then recanted the story of how he and Deja met, and they both asked, but can you trust her? Peter replied, "with my life. You just witnessed, that right?" But how do you know that P? Peter said, sometimes you can't explain, I just feel like I know. After reflecting back on all that had happened within 24 hours and she was still here, cooking or just still here, period! he was impressed. The news came on, and the men turn to the large projector screen on the wall and watched. Deja had heard the last part of the conversation and was glowing with pride for Peter. No one had ever stood up for me, much less spoke highly of me. Not even my foster mom, when I told her at eight years old, my foster dad was putting his nasty cigarette tongue on me in places that were marked private; this is what led to the gas leak that killed them both one winter night. As the crew sat and watched the news of the day. Not knowing of exactly all the damages done until it aired, but no other lives were taken but those that came for one of the F.B.I.

The next day the men were up early painting and changing key marks to the vehicles used in the shooting from the previous day. Even modifying the body styles and VIN numbers. I was beyond speechless and in awe of all the men could do. I was intrigued by them and wanted to learn more. The grounds seem to have everything possibly needed to stay there without leaving there for anything; from farm animals to an almost fully stocked local store with vegetables. From the acres of fruit and vegetables growing outside, also with a gas station, private jet and many other luxuries.

As I walked around the beautiful estate, I would guess it to be about sixty thousand square feet. With the sixteen bedrooms and eight bathrooms, a bowling alley with six lanes, also indoor basketball, ping pong, a game room the size of Dave and Busters, Peter had several very high-tech labs, and many doors that didn't open. It was a fortress, but the beauty of it made you think it was kids running around or riding the various 4-wheeler or jet skis, and other crazy looking street objects I saw on the land. I had been walking in deep thought, for some time when I came upon a stream surrounded by fruit trees and flowers, that looked like a painting that would be hanging in a museum.

I was such a Tomboy that I started to climb a tree. I was looking down on the water, and then made a comfortable spot where I just laid down, in the crest of a huge branch. I had been asleep for over an hour. The dreams of my past came to me like yesterday. I could smell the breath of that ole bastard with liquor and cigars. He would sneak into my room when he wanted to because the only time, I would come out would be to eat or do chores. I could feel his rough hands parting my young legs then his snake-like tongue stroking my body. I would start to scream and cry and then my foster mom would appear in the doorway and close the door. One night after the same events happened and I cried myself to sleep, only to be awoken by a soft voice of a woman that looked very much like a grown version of myself saying, get up and run.

I was then handed an envelope. I got up and ran as fast as my little legs could carry me. I ran until the police stopped me when they blocked me from running, the envelope was long gone. I had dropped it. I jumped up when I heard a strange noise like that of a lion or a tiger. I was so surprised because until today that dream only came in bits and pieces, never making any sense to me. Peter was standing there watching me closely again. He always seemed to be staring at me. He heard my erratic breathing and wondered what she was dreaming of and crying out about. Peter said in a soft voice, you must be careful out here. He knew the area well because he did his yoga practice there.

I looked around and said this land is beautiful, what is there to be afraid of? Peter pointed and told me, them. I turned around to see several animals: A lion and cubs, also a tiger. In the sunrise, I could see a giraffe and other animals running freely. I was amazed that I didn't notice them before. Peter said what she was thinking, it's so beautiful I didn't look close enough to see. As we sat there stealing glances, we spoke of everything and nothing. I asked him, why were you in that alley at that time of the morning? He looked confused, and said, What? When we met? I shook my head and said yes? He said, to find you, I said no, we must be honest with each other; I detest a liar. Peter shook his head and said, I was looking for someone from my past, that I saw in that area earlier that day. I went jogging to clear my head and heard the commotion between you and Henry? I said to him in a defiant voice, so you weren't looking for me. He said everything happens for a reason, our paths crossed because they were supposed to, On that night, at that time and on that day. I'm a firm believer of things happening for a reason. We can either be for a reason or a season, but I want to see you and see where we go from here. I nodded because I was so consumed with emotion that I could not speak. As we walked back to the house Peter explained why he had brought the house and land and built it off the grid. He just explained that his family was killed, no details about it, but from his voice, I could feel the emotions and hurt still lingered after all this time. As we reached the house, he told me that there were paths with maps in various rooms in places that would lead me to safety on the grounds, in case of emergency.

He also warned me that the animals had been trained by Mike, so his crew could feed them, but not to trust them without one of them being within view. I was also filled in on a multitude of hidden rooms, that although lavishly adorned were everywhere within the mansion. I asked, Peter why are you telling me all this. He turned to me with his eyes now green and said because this will be your new home. I gasped and said, are you kidnapping me? he said no. You are free to go at any time but just remember our faces were just on the news last night. After a couple of days, we can move around more freely, but I want to keep you safe, and the safest place I can think of is here with me and the crew. I hadn't thought of that just like I hadn't even thought of leaving. I didn't have anyone to miss me. My little apartment was locked up tightly plus I had spent the extra money for my room. Peter told me that everything you had at the hotel had been brought here for you. I was surprised and asked, but how? Peter said, although I'm young, I make things happen. Deja didn't know that after they left the restaurant, he told his crew to go move her things out ASAP. He didn't know why, but glad he had. Luckily too, because the shootout happened right after that. Peter always trusted his gut. Deja asked why would I be in danger? Did you know those people? Why were they trying to harm us? Peter was always honest and sometimes to a fault. So, he watched how he worded his next statement. I may know something about that, but as soon as I'm sure I will fill you in on it. I nodded in agreement and stated, I will trust you until you give me a reason not to. They smiled at each other and walked to the garage.

Once they entered the garage, Mike and Death looked up. They were surprised to see them both smiling at each other like lovesick teenagers. Death said, hey, let me whip that head right quick, chose the dual. They chose a variety of things to do, from bumper race boats on Pho river, next to mini race cars on the semi-pro racetrack. Then to playing polo on the thoroughbred horses. Deja didn't know what a net worth was but if she did, she would know he had more money than three Oprah's and two Bill Gates and counting. Peter had invested well what he was left with from his family, plus he had helped his two brothers from another mother get paid. Money was like water to the crew, but they didn't show it. Coming from nothing, they valued everything they had. Later that night they all took showers and helped cook homemade veggie pizza, hot wings, lemon wings, and sweet potato fries. After multiple drinks, they all retired to different rooms. Most of them were asleep as soon as their heads hit the pillow, but some were up dreaming of the other.

CHAPTER 8

Deja was deep in thought and making a list of questions to ask Peter. I liked the name P3, but I called him Peter. I felt that our relationship was going in a different path than anybody else's. As my eyes closed, I dreamt yet again. Tap tap…May I come in? I turned over in bed and Peter came to my side and kissed my lips. I have been waiting all day long to do that. Why do you hunt me even in my awa state? I smiled and told him so do you. As we kissed more, he joined me on the king-size bed and continued to explore my body with his hands. He smelled of mint and something sweet. His mouth was everywhere like his hands. I buried my hands in his hair. Pulling him to me. When his kisses started traveling lower, I held my breath. I was panting and my head was swinging from side to side slowly. When his mouth captured my pearl tongue, I inhaled so much air it felt as if my chest was going to explode. He lapped at me like he was dying of thirst. Before a drop of my juices could hit the bed, he was there, licking and sucking it up. He was moaning or talking I didn't know which, but I knew it was driving me beyond insane. This is an area I had been violated in, but the feeling was unlike anything I had ever felt. His mouth was so wet and gentle, yet he sucked and licked with a hunger. When he added a finger, I moaned out loudly, he went in and out of me causing my legs to shake and my body to move uncontrollable. My hands were still buried in his hair. I was holding him in place. Begging for the torture to continue. When he added another finger, this time to my anus, I was in full convulsion. I was begging him to fuck me. He refused me until I screamed out his name and he only then unbuttoned his pants and massaged himself to an erect state. I was on fire. My nipples were so hard, and I had made a puddle underneath us. He got to his knees and kissed me deeply. I tasted myself. The taste of pineapples and mango with a mixture of me was on both of our lips. As he was deep throating me, he entered me with so much force that I bit his tongue. We both were in pain but not from injuries but from the pleasure we were enjoying. His tempo was as if he was listening to an old R&B song in his head. I fucked him back to the Comfort song by Shai playing in my mind. As he pulled out, I moved forward, going deeper and deeper and deeper. At first, I could not take his girth, the thickness of him, with his length, made me wet. The wetness allowed him to go deeper. As the access was approved, he drove deep into my cave hitting the walls and causing sheetrock to crash and fall. He was breaking windows and opening rooms to accommodate an open floor plan. He was now over me, pumping wildly, tearing me in good ways, I was caught up now and by him. With his arms locked in place, I could only wrap my legs around him and hold on. We both felt like we were on fire, I had a sensation like I had to urinate. I told Peter; I have to pee. He started kissing me, and told me in between breaths, no sweet baby, you are Cumming. The slow smile that crept up on his face was priceless. Peter slowed his pace and almost completely stopped. But I could feel him pulsating within me still. My breathing had almost returned to normal. When he hit me harder and pumped into me another couple of times, I screamed out while my body shook uncontrollably. He watched as I bit my lip, only then did he raised my legs above my head, with one hand holding me in place. Peter went balls deep inside of me. My eyes were squeezed tightly shut. I could feel his dick fucking me. The love making was gone he was literally fucking the shit out of me, but the sensation of his balls slapping into me caused me to raise up off the bed, arms and legs wrapped around him for dear life. I rode him like a horse. I was soaking wet; his hair was plastered to me. He was now sitting on his ass and I was over him. Peter grabbed my hips and made me take all of him. His arms were holding me from the back in place, while he hit my love spot repeatedly. Both of us were spent and coming completely undone. Peter had been holding his climax since he first entered me and although I had already cum, I was about to cum again. We both exploded and saw rockets and galaxies pass. As we came down, we were wrapped in each other arms. The sounds of birds woke me up, and my hand was between my legs. Waking up again soaking wet. I looked around and smiled to myself and said, damn girl, we've got to get some of that with a girlish giggle. I was a virgin still. So, these dreams were surreal, and much needed to say the least, I wanted Peter like I wanted and needed air.

CHAPTER 9

Deja peered out of the window over the gorgeous estate. My breath caught, but not from the estate view, but from the owner of the estate, doing some kind of a slow dance that looked like, he was fighting and dancing at the same time. I just stayed in place for a few moments, watching his limbs move with a fluent skill. Peter wasn't moving fast but the sweat on his body made him look like he had just swum miles in Pho river. His hair was down around his face blowing in the wind. He had so many tattoos all over his chest and back, there were faces and animals, but it looked like it was telling a story. As he turned slowly the pictures had my mind reeling. He also had many marks on his body that looked like at one time he could have been hurt.

When I realized that he might have been hurt before I covered my mouth and moved away from the window. It was too late; Peter had already seen me. He continued to do his exercise because he had a daily ritual. Once I moved away from the window, I took a seat on the bed. I had a lot of things to weigh in on. The last couple of hours was like a whirlwind, but I had been the happiest I had been in years. I went into the bathroom that was almost as big as my whole apartment and I touched everything. The gold faucets with the various vanilla, lavender, and rosewater scents. The marble countertops with the double sinks that were big enough for me to take a bath in. The mirrors were so big I could see my whole body in them. The water from the clawfoot tub started to fog up the bathroom. As I sunk into the tub, I pushed a button and a 50-inch T.V. dropped down from the ceiling. A space that looked like an opening in the wall became a beautiful gas fireplace. On the T.V. I selected "'Just Like Me" by Jamie Fox. As I went under the water, I wanted to wash my whole body of my past and all the wrong life had handed me to date. I soaked for what seemed like hours.

When I finally emerged for air, I rose out of the tub. As I looked at myself in the mirror, I took in every mark, every curve. I just realized that I had no clothes to wear for the day. As a matter of fact, the clothes I was wearing were the only clothes I had, since someone had broken into my apartment and stole everything that wasn't too big to carry. That night I was in the alley was because I was afraid to go home. I had to get my rent money but just knowing someone had been through all my stuff and then to steal personal items, I was puzzled. As I dried myself with a 1000% cotton towel I was in heaven.

The sheets had to be a million thread I thought as I rubbed my body dry. Everything was so top of the line. I thought; let me sneak down the hall to Peter's room and get a T-shirt and maybe some sweats or some basketball shorts. When I walked into Peter's bedroom my mouth was opened so wide my throat went dry. His room was maybe 2500 sq. feet. everything was so shiny and new. The room had all shades of cream and blue with a hint of purple and mint green. The ceiling was painted like a beautiful museum wall with tiny sparkling lights. It looked like a piece of art. He had several Plasma HD T.Vs on one wall with

The News playing in different languages. The floors were a rich deep wood that looked like mahogany, with thick plush rugs in various places. The other wall was from the floor to ceiling windows. With a view of the river and trees, you could see the animals through it. It almost looked like you were outside in the forest. The huge chandelier over the bed looked as if you could swing on it like monkey bars. He had so many books. When I turned around, I saw an 8ft. wine room that was next to a fireplace that I could stand in comfortably.

I started walking toward the sound of the music, Peter was rapping; she's the type of chick that you can't live without, take her home and let her meet your momma, won't trip when your phone rings off the hook, Ain't with that extra drama. Overlook the fact that sometimes you don't know how to act…Damn! He's rapping my favorite song Wife her by

"Sekay." As the water slid off his body he was lathered up. The smell coming from the restroom seemed to follow him. The smell of him was sweet and intoxicating. I just watched as he shook the water from his hair. His hands rubbed water over his body slowly rising off the soap. Now she could see everything clearly. He was beautiful his whole body was chiseled like a Greek statue. As he barely washed himself, his muscles in his arms ripped like he was flexing. He was standing still but the water was happy dancing off his body.

The dreams she had was nothing compared to his actual body. His manhood wasn't erect, but she would have to cover it with two hands. His legs were strong and cut, only one leg had tats on it. The other leg was completely covered. His body told a story. She wanted him to tell her exactly what the story was about. Was this why Death and Mike asked could he trust her? She looked up and he saw her.

She just waved hey and mouthed I'm sorry. As she left the room with a towel on, she had forgotten all about the clothes she once needed. She ran back to her room. After about ten minutes she heard a knock on the door. When she said enter, Peter stuck his head in the door and Smiling he said hey Lil peeper, I didn't know you were a peeping Tom. He laughed and she threw a pillow at him. They both laughed, Deja smiled and said I'm sorry. I'm really sorry. Peter said, don't say you are sorry or apologize for something if given the chance to do again you would. Deja said, right, right, then I'm not sorry.

Damn boy, you know you are fine right? He said, is that why you were staring at me? She thought for a second and said hell yea. He said, good, I'm glad you didn't lie. I detest liars. If you keep it real with me, I will do the same with you. Did you need something? She said oh yeah, I needed a shirt and some sweats if you can spare some. Peter said, cool, just go into my room and get whatever you need. Deja said thank you.

As they both left her room Peter told her, make sure you put on something you can go out in. Oh, where am I going sir? You are going to the mall, I need some things, maybe you can help me get super fly like you. Boy stop, you know you've got extra fucking swag. As they walked back into Peter's room, Deja asked, who decorated this place for you. He said, to be honest, it's close to how my mom had our house decorated when I was a kid. Deja said your home must have been very beautiful. He said it was. As she walked through the bathroom and realized how huge it was Deja said these rooms are so large. Peter told her I wanted it to feel like it did when I was a kid. Wow, was all Deja could say.

CHAPTER 10

eath and Mike were in the kitchen. As Peter and Deja entered, they greeted, sup fam. Everybody spoke and Deja asked Peter what the hell is that? They were two robots in the kitchen, one was cooking and the other was serving food. They looked like real people, even the skin looked real, Both De'Ann and Russell had red eyes and if I didn't see them, I would never have realized they weren't real people. The male robot looked like he was kin to Peter and the female robot had long locks with a huge smile on her face. They were cooking bacon, eggs, pancakes, waffles, French toast and grits. There were 3 different machines on the counter making coffee, tea and cappuccino.

The female robot was washing dishes. Deja asked, how? How is all this happening? She's a robot, her hands are in the water? Peter said, this is my family, I created them to live as a human would. They can function as we do on a day to day basis. Death and Mike were laughing so hard they had tears in their eyes. They had been around so long, that nothing Peter created surprised them plus Russell and De'Ann had been around for years. Whenever I'm away, they make sure the grounds are kept up. They care for the animals and oversee the grounds. As they sat down and ate, the robots served them and cleaned the area. They even held conversations and could keep up with the crew on current situations.

Deja didn't know they had weapon training and were equipped with several high-tech weapons on them. Peter asked the guys if they wanted to ride to the mall. Everyone said yea in unison. After they ate, they went to the garage and got in a dark blue suburban and drove out. The windows were dark on the truck but not illegal tint. The Galleria mall was packed. They were able to move through the mall without anyone bothering them or noticing them. They went from store to store, different luxury stores.

They went from Gucci, to Prada, to Sunglass Hut. In every store, they dropped stacks, so many stacks that they could have bought a nice home and car. If she looked at something it was put in a bag. If he thought, she would like something he bought it. Peter bought her more clothes than she owned in her life. Russell had disappeared after they went into what could have been their 10th or 15th store. They had shopped themselves hungry. They all agreed on steak and seafood. As they walked around the corner to the well-known restaurant, that feeling Peter got came on strong.

He started looking around and didn't notice anyone strange. As soon as he looked at De'Ann, her eyes were no longer hazel brown but red and solid. He knew she had been activated. He had installed a facial recognition software on her and Russell, that would record faces and conversations of people in the area that were in their same space multiple times. Russell had left to go and take the bags home but sent the armored car back that resembled a Telsa in a truck form to go and get them. The truck was awaiting their arrival in the parking lot.

CHAPTER 11

They finished eating but the conversation had changed to talks of cars and sports. The guys kept speaking and then arguing over Texans, Dallas, and Pittsburgh. They were like big kids, they even played rock paper scissors for the bill. The bill for the food was almost $700.00. They all chose rock at the end and then put their black cards in Mike's fitted cap. I got to pick the winner; it was Death. I noticed none of the men had bags, they all seemed to have vanished while they are laughing and walking briskly, almost so fast that I was jogging.

De'Ann was walking behind us all, talking on the phone like she was enjoying a conversation with one of her girlfriends. She looked like the cool aunt that was along for the ride with her favorite nieces and nephews. She wore dark sunshades and a nice wide brim hat. Her stylish clothes were beautiful and spelt wealth. Why do they keep talking about sports? Again, Death won the argument. We were about four stores from the exit, and someone threw a chair.

That chair slammed into the wall right next to us. A group of men started to fight in front of them. The crew started surrounding me. With De'Ann in the rear, I was covered like the president by the secret service. A couple of men start charging at the crew and all hell broke loose. They were fighting two to three men at once, each one of them was handling their own. De'Ann was leading me out of the mall. I turned around to see Mike kicking a man in the head. Death had a man in the headlock and punching him in the nose. Peter was swinging on several men at once. As we got into the hallway, the men were heading to the car with what looked like a mob of men following them.

Once I was placed in the car, De'Ann took off down the hall like Robocop, she was running almost faster than I could see. Once the crew was out of the way, her body created something that looked like a door blocking the path of the other men. Once all the men were safely inside, I saw her go back to a female form running toward the car. No one was in the driver seat, yet the car was driving in the parking garage. Once they got down to the third level of the parking garage. A white car shot out in front of them.

The truck ramped it like a toy car. The car flew in the air. Next, I saw 2 men that looked like they were Asian running towards us with guns. The crew was sitting back talking like nothing was going on even though outside the truck looked like an action-adventure movie. I continued to look outside and saw more bloodshed when the truck rammed a man in between two cars, then something that sounded like a vacuum came out from under the car and retrieved the bodies.

Next, I heard bullets flying and hitting the truck, the crew was still talking and laughing. I screamed, what the hell is going on? They looked at me and laughed. Death said, Lil lady, we are at war. But why are you guys sitting back, laughing and chilling like nothing is wrong? We trust our creation to know that we are safe. Just as the truck pulled out of the parking garage, De'Ann jumped back into the truck. Taking off her hat and shaking all the bullets out of her hair. Deja nearly passed out. It was too much going on around her. She didn't know why but the men were too comfortable with the violence and that was truly scary.

CHAPTER 12

As they drove down the highway near their home, Deja noticed that Russell had joined them, he was now following the truck in the suburban from earlier. He had dark glasses on as well as De'Ann. It seemed they were going a different way from the first-time home. This view was beautiful as well, but no other cars were on this highway. I didn't ask any questions because I knew I was protected. As we went under a bridge the highway turned into what looked like a mining area. The sunlight became nighttime. I looked back and saw what looked like a huge door closed after we entered something that looked like a cave.

I had to ask one question though, excuse me guys, what was all the sports talk about. All of them started speaking at once. Peter took the lead. Well, we knew we were in a little jam so to speak. So, we were trying to see who had to shoot first or take the first punch. The crew laughed, we know it's kind of twisted but as you get to know us you will see, so are we. What was that with the opening of the ground back there? Well, if we were being followed, we aren't anymore. Peter owns the property, once we got to that part of the land, so we came into the house via the underground. Mike said, you will get used to all the gadgets but if you see something strange that you don't understand, don't be afraid to ask. As they reached another part of the underground pathway, she started seeing animals, and pictures on the walls of various things from water, to birds, to karate men fighting, to families walking in the park at the beach. There was a herd of goats in the way and Mike made a funny noise and they parted like a quick weave bob with a part. This day just kept on getting better. As an opening became visible, De'Ann jumped out and paced the area. I looked at her and noticed that one of her arms had become a machine gun. The garage was immaculate, wow again.

They walked through a cascade of water or something that looked like water. As soon as they got close to the waterfall it would stop, to allow entry in the house. First, you had to pass by a beach scene equipped with sand and a volleyball net even a firepit. There were palm trees, several hammocks, and huge windows, that opened to jet skis as well as a yacht, all of this under the house or mansion. I smelt something like spicy seafood. As we got into the kitchen it was a spread of all kinds of seafood, a huge seafood boil was thrown all over the table with corn, potatoes, mushrooms, turkey necks. A pot of gumbo was cooking with cornbread on the stove with dirty rice and jambalaya. Everyone walked in and washed their hands. We sat down to eat and the talking and laughter was something that I have never experienced. If this was what a real family felt like I wanted this every day and all the time. We decided on trying to do Karaoke. We chose to do it in the bowling alley, the acoustics was great. The music was loud, and Peter had several microphones so we could do a backup on other people's song as they sang. First up was Death, his selection was DeBarge "Time Will Reveal." The Crew was his backup, it was so funny how all these dudes dressed like thugs and singing in soft tones. What can I do to make you feel secure? Move all your doubts so that you will know for sure that you are the apple of my eye girl. Fulfillment of my dreams. This was supposed to be Karaoke, but Deja was in a daze listening to the words. She had never heard a song like this, the words were spellbinding. I know just how you feel, but this time the love is for real. She was crying at the end. Will allllll reveeeeal in time.

I had to wipe my face before anyone noticed it. Next was a song that De'Ann sang, the person's name was Vanessa Williams. Sometimes the snow comes down in June and sometimes the sun goes around the moon. I see the passion in your eye, sometimes it's all a big surprise. These songs were so intense I was in deep thought. I heard some upbeat music and then Russell's voice, Candy girl you are all my world. Then the crew jumped in, screaming Candy…. candy girl, it was hilarious. They pulled me up and the rest of the night I learned new songs and even some moves from everybody. We danced until we were soaking wet. We ended that night cooking smores by the fire pit that was in the ground and covered with different colored rocks that sparkled as the fire burned. For the next two months, we shopped, ate out, even flew to different places. I had been to so many places, and learned so many things, that it seemed as if I was growing and changing into a person that was cultured. We flew to New York just to shop and then The Crew taught me how to ice skate. Then we saw a play with Toni Braxton on Broadway. I even went to Times Square where we danced and celebrated nothing special but life with others in a line dance fashion. I still would go to Wal-Mart and shop, but Peter would not allow me to go anywhere alone. Me and De'Ann got so close that it was like having a big sister. As we were walking back to Death condo in New York. Peter pulled me to the side and asked me for a date. We had been around everyone for so long. It just took me aback that he asked me out alone. I asked him where we were going, and he said just be patient you will see later tonight. Deja didn't know if this was a good idea or not because her feelings for Peter had surpassed love, she was head over heels in love with him. They had never touched beyond a kiss here and there, but her dreams had her wanting more, much more. Peter had dreams of his own that consumed him of Deja. He had never made love before or thought of it after his past.

CHAPTER 13

Once Deja arrived back at the condo. She was shocked, when she walked into the bedroom she was staying in and noticed that it was filled with different flowers. Some she didn't really know of any flowers by name but the rose. The room smelled of expensive perfume. The bed was incased with flowers. The bathroom had flowers on the counters and floors. The tub was filled with rose petals and other flowers. The water was a rich bed of watercolors and smelled of honey and melon. There where candles burning everywhere, some in glass cases others sitting on candle holders with what looked like mini chandeliers hanging from them. The music was softly playing in the background. Some lady was purring in the background about sweet love. As I climbed into the sunken tub, the water was just the right temperature hot. I had long ago stopped asking Peter how he did something to surprise me. The whole family would be out enjoying entertainment and I would get a text from him or a love letter throughout the day and we would be standing right next to each other. We both knew how we felt about each other in just days it seemed. I just didn't know why we had not acted on our feelings. As soon as

I stepped out of the tub. I wrapped myself in a rose-colored fluffy towel. I heard music playing from the other room and when I walked into my bedroom, I saw three very nice dressed women standing in my room. One of the women was laying jewelry out on this midnight blue velvet cloth on the bed, the other woman was going through a rack of what looked like designer gowns with beautiful colorful beading and crystals. There were shoes and purses to match every gown. The other lady was warming what looked like a lotion she had next to a massage table. She told me to remove the towel and get on the table. I was fast asleep until I was shaken back to consciousness and asked what dress would I like to wear? The layouts of clothes and shoes were placed around the room so that I could see the difference in each. The last lady started on my nails; a beige French manicure was added. We added shoes and jewelry to the attire. Just as I was about to get dressed, two other women appeared in my room and looked at my outfit and ushered me to a chair. One started doing my hair and makeup, it was crazy. They applied foundations, eyelashes, blushes and all kinds of beautiful color to my eyelids. All the attention was on me. I didn't know if he thought I was ugly, or if he wanted to spoil me. I didn't care, I was enjoying it all. Once I was dressed, the women excused themselves. I could only stand in the floor-length mirror and look at myself. Meanwhile, Peter was in his bedroom getting dressed. He was told of Deja's dress choice and wanted to match with her. He took extra time getting dressed because this was his very first date. The way he did everything for Deja you would think he was an experienced dater or someone that had done this a million times. Her dress choice was a gold dress with cream shoes, gold and diamond jewels to match. The beaded purse was also a great match. Her hair was pulled into an updo style with kiss curls draping down near her ears. Since she really didn't like makeup, the makeup artist was excellent. Her skin was so smooth. The hints of gold color on her eyes and the bronze color on her cheeks made her look as if she was glowing. She felt like a princess. As Peter turned to the mirror. He was impressed with himself. He had his silk locks pulled back in a man bun. He had a five o'clock shadow with a goatee that was trimmed nicely. He didn't wear much jewelry, but he did wear an ankh ring with diamonds on it. A nice Turkish link chain, with a picture of his mom and dad a month before they were killed. He checked his watch and walked into the living room. Just as he was coming into view, he looked up and saw Deja walking down the stairs. He froze in his footsteps. She was gorgeous. The crew walked in and went completely silent, watching the exchange between Deja and Peter was breathtaking. It was like watching a soon to be husband await his new bride to be, walking down the aisle to join him in his new life. Russell informed them that the car was waiting outside. As she walked down the stairs, his breath was caught in his chest and he had to remind himself to breathe. He sent all the people to help her because he didn't want her to worry, or stress over anything, not over her hair, clothes or anything at all.

CHAPTER 14

As they left the condo, Deja asked, where are we going? Peter was still staring at her. She blushed; you are so beautiful. Thank you, you are very handsome yourself Mr. Man. They spoke and laughed as they passed many sights. Peter loved history and told her of the history of each building as they drove around the city, she was given a crash course in the city of New York story. When they approached a pier, there was a yacht waiting for them. Once they got aboard, a beautiful table was set up with crystal glasses, candles and chilled champagne, it was lovely. She looked up to see two very large feet standing in front of her, she veered up and noticed they were in front of the statue of liberty. She looked at Peter concerned, and he smiled, and all her doubt was wiped clean. He told her to remove her shoes. And he got down on one knee and replaced her shoes with something that looked like ballerina slippers. His touch was so kind and comforting. As they walked up steps it seemed like every twenty steps, he would turn to her and kiss her each time more passionately. There were still a lot of steps from the top when he told her from here, we will take the elevator. She said so why didn't we take the elevator to begin with. We didn't take the elevator to start with because I want you to know as the times get harder, I will be there to love you and kiss you always. As we climb together nothing will get harder because we can figure it out. Simple is not our way but we'll always fly higher together. She was in tears, the most basic thing to others, she had thought it to be a grand romantic jester. As soon as the elevator opened, she could see the view over New York from the statue's crown. As she walked around the crown witnessing the view, a buffet was set up with a chef cooking on a hibachi grill. There was prime rib, lobster, scallops, sweet potatoes and salad with fresh fruit and finger sandwiches. We were served while watching the city all around us. Even though the city was so alive, I only noticed the man before me. Music was playing after dinner and Peter asked her to dance with him. "Hope" came on by Jagged Edge followed by "Overdose" by Jamie Foxx, the songs were so fitting. After they left the statue of liberty, they went to a beach nearby. They walked on the beach and splashed water on each other. They did not care about the labels they wore. They saw a lighthouse nearby and went to explore it closer. As they were walking, Deja started picking up shells on the beach, she explained that she never had a chance to do this while growing up, so Peter assisted her with her task. Peter was so much fun. Deja had seen many faces of Peter from the intellectual businessman to the wheeler and dealer in reality, to the exchange of stocks in the stock market. At first, Deja really had believed him to be a drug dealer; from all the violence going on around him, to the smart home with the crazy security. Just the way he moved in her hood. He commanded respect. Peter commanded respect everywhere he went. Every city they would visit he would treat everyone with respect. He was as nice as he was a killer. She always felt so at peace with him. She just knew he was the type of man that would protect her. Peter told Deja, you got dirt on your face and splashed water on her. She gave chase but Peter was fast, as he ran, he was stripping out of his clothes and by the time she reached him, he had on midnight blue silk boxers. She got down to her bra and panties and they matched his. She ran to the water and dove in. They played more on the beach, once the wind picked up and it got chilly, they remembered the lighthouse. They gathered their clothes and ran towards the light coming from the water. When we approached the house, Peter wrapped his jacket around her shoulders, he then told her to wait outside the house until he checked it out. He went around the back of the house and broke a window to enter. He cracked a couple of windows open on the way to the door. When he opened the door, Deja was shaking from the night chill. He led her to the stove which he lit and opened the oven to get it warm in the house. Once they ventured around and examined the lighthouse. It had been newly redone like a very stylish loft. There were exposed wooden beams over the ceiling. The fireplace was gas, it had wood in a container next to it. He didn't know where the light switch was, so he lit candles everywhere. Their silhouette was beautiful on the grey colored walls. The lighthouse was decorated in bright bold colors. After exploring the property, they realized it was a three-bedroom with a two and a half baths. The kitchen was huge with lots of space. Deja went into one bathroom and Peter went into the other. As they returned to the common area in the living room, they gravitated toward one another, they just held each other and swayed in place. Peter walked her into the bedroom, as they laid down on the bed and spooned, they fell asleep in each other arms. A couple of hours later, Deja was awakened by Peter's anguished cries in his sleep. His arms and legs were very stiff. His breathing was very shallow, and his body was wet from perspiring. His chest stuck out like someone was holding him down by his arms and legs. As Deja called his name softly, he didn't reply. She was in fear of waking him up abruptly.

CHAPTER 15

eter had three women licking and touching him everywhere. He was so afraid to move, the woman in black leather or mistress, as she liked to be called was barking out orders. Fuck them harder, and you better not cum! Sit on his face! Lick his nipples, you must fuck her harder! Thrust your hips into her more and grind! She burned him with a cigarette. Slower and harder she said in a sinister tone. Why are you not listening to me? She burned him again with a hot poker from the fireplace and he screamed out from the pain. He smelt his skin burning, the smell turned his stomach. The mistress screamed! All of you get up and go to the other side of the room. The mistress was referring to the ladies and teen girls in the room. You, she pointed a skinny finger referring to Peter. Lay your ass back down. She had been fucking all the other young boys under the age of sixteen years old all day. She walked over and told four young women to hold Peter down, right before she opened her legs and lowered herself down on his shaft, She told him, you better not go soft, you will fuck me until I cum. Her center was so dry, it felt like he was getting stabbed by small needles in his genitals. She forced her nipples in and out of his mouth, this seems to give Peter some relief, as she got a little moister, She would literally raise all the way up off him to drop down on him with all her weight, sometimes knocking the wind out of his small body. He had been a sex slave for rich women for over a year now. His body had started to change and look trimmer and more cut from all the sexing exercises and lifting daily. When he didn't perform well to a client's liking, he was severely beaten and punished. Peter was very good at fighting but trying to fight three or four grown men at one time was not an option. His body couldn't handle the blows. He had tried to run often and was beaten within an inch of his life, only to be healed and punished again. He tried to please the clients the way they asked, so no beatings would come or if his body was too bruised, they wouldn't feed him. Too many clients would ask questions but not help him. They just didn't want to look at the scars but wanted the sex. But regardless of the hurt, his body felt he had to work daily, sometimes for ten hours straight, he would fuck various rich women and their daughters. Some would even have him stay at their home with their kids and say he was their kids' friend so their husbands wouldn't get suspicious. Peter had been one of the favorites and known to be a moneymaker. He brought in thousands daily. With his good looks and shy personality, it drew the women to him. He was also 6-foot-tall at 14 years old. As the mistress fucked him raw, he could feel his manhood bleeding from the harsh treatment of her genitals handling him so roughly. The mistress had over fifty young men working in different states. She would also take pictures and record the sexual acts with the women for blackmail purposes if she didn't get her way from her clients. Peter had slept with presidents' wives and even minsters wives for the mistress. As the mistress now had him fucking her from the back he was about to blackout from the pain and not getting enough nutrients. She was throwing her ass back on him so hard causing it to feel like his skin was being ripped off. He heard one of the women in the room yell out! "You're a dirty little bastard, the client was screaming, he erupted on my back and in my hair." The mistress raised up from Peter and dismissed him, but not before she told him to rub his load out. He was standing in front of her while she beat him across the back with a horsewhip. He was bleeding and wet from his sweat, the pain was so unbearable he could hardly stand. If she didn't catch the nut no one else would. Although they would have to rub their seeds out, they were not allowed to enjoy the sexual acts or to get anyone pregnant. After Peter relieved himself, he was then dragged out of the room. He was tied to the steel bars that the young men were handcuffed to at night, so they could not run away. As Deja called to him, he heard her and tried to wake up but not before he reached out and grabbed Deja's neck roughly. She was gasping for air when she slapped him hard, he woke up crying and released her immediately. He was so sorry he couldn't apologize enough. The look of horror in Deja's eyes scared him. He got up out of bed and dressed only in his boxers and a t-shirt and left the lighthouse. After hours of running on the beach. He returned to hearing Deja crying. He remained outside for some time until he heard nothing. When he walked back into the lighthouse, she still had fresh tears on her face asleep. He felt like his heart was pulled from his chest with dull scissors and cut into small pieces. These nightmares had caused him not to share his bed with anyone. And now he had hurt Deja.

CHAPTER 16

Deja woke up to a smell that caused her mouth to salivate. As she opened her eyes, she could see Peter standing at the stove shirtless. She could watch him forever. The tattoos on his back looked like people screaming. Their mouths were open, and some faces were twisted like they were in pain. Deja rose up out of bed slowly but yawned with more sound than was needed because she would never sneak up on him again. She noticed there were fried fish, grits, eggs and toast with cold orange juice on the counter. As she bit into a piece of toast, she asked Peter cautiously not wanting to upset him. Where did you get all this food from? Peter told her there was an orange tree behind the lighthouse as well as a farm. So, he got the eggs from the farmer and picked the fruit from the trees in the back. He caught two fish while he was out jogging, and the grits and bread were in the cabinet. She was amazed, Peter had never cooked before in front of her in the months they had known each other. Mainly I guess because he had staff to do so. The food was even better than it smelled. As we finished eating breakfast, I asked him was he okay? He smiled and told me Yes, I'm doing better than I have been in a long time. We found a chess set and he taught me to play. After he finally let me win, I quit while I was on a high. We played cards and other games, we even played Marco Polo in the ocean. We acted as if we were two teenagers running wild with no parents to control us and no outside world existed. As the sun went down, we fished and caught crab and shrimp. We even feasted on fresh tuna and avocado toast that we picked from the nearby farm, he was an amazing chef. We sat out by the fire covered in a blanket just holding each other. As it got colder, we went into the house. We had a jam session from the music playlist on our phones and it was a collection of our favorite R&B songs; we had a similar taste, we both liked to listen to the lyrics of music, it was very profound, just being able to listen to music and letting the music speak for you. Then we started telling stories of our childhood, the fun and laughter times we enjoyed. I couldn't remember too many, but I always remembered my mom telling me; I love you more than all the angels in heaven, and beyond that. Peter then told me of how his parents died, and how he lived in a house for many days with dead bodies and body parts all over the house, he told me of how he dragged them outside. Then dug holes on his family land to bury them and he did all this without being caught by the Triads nightly for weeks. The story that caused my heart to break was when he told me of how he had made it all the way to the United States, alone only to get thrown into a child sex trafficking ring a year after being in America. He then told me of how he was treated by the many rich women. The sexual acts he discussed with me were horrible, they made my stomach churn. His virginity was taken from him by force when he refused to have sex with a senator's daughter in the presence of the senator, his wife and the sex mistress at gunpoint. He was beaten severely and scarred. We spoke so freely and about so much. We both cried and held onto each other for our dear lives. It seemed our young lives had been so horrible to us both. We made a vow to change that. We started kissing and touching each other and before we knew it, he was between my legs devouring me. It felt so much better than my dreams. I was so wet from the noises he was making while sucking on my sunshine between my legs, it was driving me over the edge of insanity. He was rubbing my breast as he hungrily ate my flower. He ran his hands down the inside of my thighs and caused my body to shake and tremble. He was a skilled lover to say the least. Once he got over me. My body froze up and I started to cry, I explained to him that I was still a virgin and he refused to enter me. He dropped down on his knees and started to devour me again, my body was having spasms, I could no longer take the pleasure and he allowed me to return from heaven slowly. Once I was back on earth, I tried to relieve him, but he would not allow me to. He said his job was to please me and when the time came, we would experience each other on all levels. Peter wanted both of their first times to be memorable. He would consider her to be his first, if they got that far. She would be the first he would give himself to with his consent willingly.

CHAPTER 17

The next morning waking up to another wonderful breakfast, this time in bed. Peter was so loving, kind and the way he held me and looked at me when speaking to me was amazing. We had just finished cleaning up the lighthouse. When Russell and De'Ann knocked on the door. They brought us more clothes and they also came to pick us up. While we showered, Russell repaired the broken window, everything had been repaired to a perfect state even the love between Peter and Deja. We both knew we were in love with each other, but with our past would it be a lock against us or help unlock the life waiting for us. Now she knew why he wouldn't touch her. Why it seemed he would never sleep. Why he loved his family and catered to everyone around him. Peter knew why she didn't want to wear a dress or appear too attractive. It was because she thought it was a tease to men or caused men to rape women. Both of their issues were caused by other people. To talk and air out the dirty laundry of their ghost-past formed a bond between the two. On the way back home, Deja and Peter were on a high. De'Ann and Russell were on high alert. They had noticed some strange behavior. People at the beach supposedly riding bikes but was walking the bikes instead of riding them. Bird watchers having binoculars, but no birds present. The same couples in the cars close by, watching them and not the road or studying maps upside down. They made it to the block prior to stopping at Deaths' condo, by now Peter noticed the multiple times they had hit corners, he was alert and on point as he laughed with Deja. She sensed the change and hugged him as they got out of the car, Russell had given him a gun and he passed it to Deja. Over the last couple of months, he had trained her daily on hand to hand fighting techniques and shooting weapons, now she knew why. They never knew if it was the Triads, the sex ring or if it was people, they had blackmailed for the sex traffickers, but they always knew to be on alert. A lady bumped into Deja so hard she almost knocked her down. Deja recovered quickly but not before she felt the taser hitting her in her chest. She saw the strings, but it still felt like a heart attack. As she went down, she heard shots being fired. The last face she saw was Peter's he was trying to fight off several people. Russell and De'Ann were in full war mode. Their eyes were blazing red and their arms had turned into machine guns. Then an explosion happened and separated them. She saw a net that looked like it was electrocuting them and holding them down to the ground with spikes. They were smoking and their skin was melting off. Deja woke up in a very posh hotel or home she didn't know which. The bed smelled of lavender and vanilla were very strong. There was an older lady sitting in a chair next to the bed. She was reading the Art of War. Well, hello young lady? Deja jumped when she realized there were armed guards in the room with her as well. She was in a beautiful powdered blue gown. Deja was silent because Peter told her if something like this happened to remain calm, he would always come for her, but she didn't know where he was or if he was okay. The older lady was the first to speak, "If you do as I ask you won't be harmed, but if you choose to try me you will regret it and may suffer my wrath. I will allow you to rest now but when I come back you will speak to me voluntarily or involuntarily. Good night dear. Deja felt a small pinch and her eyes closed. As she slept her dreams were hunted by nightmares. She was a little girl running in a nightgown barefoot down the street, her foster dad was chasing her, the faster she ran the closer he got. She woke up screaming Peter's name, she heard laughter and then the same voice said sweetheart he's not coming. That sinister laugh was heartbreaking. Deja felt a tear fell as she was put under again. Meanwhile, Death and Mike were tearing up the streets of New York trying to find out what happened to half of their family. They both agreed not to leave the city until they found their brother and newfound sister. Russell and De'Ann were found on the street in a nearby alley by people thinking they were terminator dolls that went bad from a movie set. The media's narrative was always something fake or made up because they never knew the facts or tried to ask. The news reported several people died that day but no word of Deja or Peter. They didn't know if Deja was dead or alive. They did know that Peter had no fingerprints as a result of being burnt off while being tortured years ago while they were in the sex ring. This made them think of their first meeting as young boys. This was one of the ways they were punished for not performing successfully, meaning if they burst a nut or faked like enjoying the deed and the client didn't feel satisfied, they were punished. One night many years ago, three young men were placed in a van together. One was taken from a hospital. He was still in a hospital gown with no clothes or shoes on. He had fresh blood on him, this was Peter. He looked as if he was very confused as to where he was. He didn't cry but he looked like he wanted to. The other young man had been taken from a juvenile unit in Dallas, TX, this was (Deleon) Death. He was badly bruised as well and very thin. He looked like he had not eaten in days. The last one to enter the van looked like he had been taken out of the woods, this was Mike; he only had on ripped shorts like the character the incredible hulk after he changed. Mud was all over him. You could barely see his eyes. All the boys were hogged tied and gagged. They could only stare at each other. As the night turned into day, they were transferred like cattle from one means of transportation to another. They had been traveling for days and was only allowed to go to the restroom twice a day, they were fed just enough to say they ate but not enough to give them the energy to move around. On what they counted, or thought was day six, they were drugged and when they woke up, they were in a room where there were beds in a room that looked like a dorm of a prison. It was clean but the lights were so bright and there were so many other boys there.

CHAPTER 18

They woke up at 3 A.M. to do chores, whatever chores were allotted to them must be done and no arguing or changing schedule between each other. They never knew where each other were going from day to day. The young men were fed breakfast around 8 am, then they had to go to work. Usually working out first because that was imperative to have their bodies tone. They were weighed daily to make sure no one was sneaking food or was given over the allotted amount of food. After they showered, they were dressed in suits that looked like they came off the runway in Paris. Our hair was trimmed as well as our nails cut. We were paraded in front of women and men like show ponies. We had numbers on our lapel and bets were made on each one of us, the highest bidder was rewarded with sex from that prize. The new kids' bids were the highest. Some broke the bank. Peter was the first ever to get a 1-million-dollar bid. Mike was next at $856,000. After the auction, we were split up and taken to a room or hotel to be raped. Peter told us on his first night he was made to have sex with the mother and three daughters. After the three daughters were broken in as they called it, being broken in is a term used after having sex and your virginity is no longer intact. Peter had to perform everything from anal sex to oral sex on all the daughters. The mother watched and issued out commands to Peter and her daughters. She continually yelled out; you better learn how to fuck, or you will soon run out of luck, all the while laughing. Peter had to have sex with their mother next. She made her daughters watch her and Peter as she explained to them how to work their hips. She then showed them how to have oral sex, she licked Peter until he was red and swollen. Once the guards showed up to take him back to the compound, he was thrown out of the room naked and told he needed work. He was then beaten with a bamboo stick until he couldn't stand. The woman was told by the mistress he would be returning to satisfy her again once he got coached. When he arrived back at the compound, he was locked up like a caged animal and made to have sex several times a day under the guidance of a sex coach. Peter had never had sex before that night, so he didn't know what he was doing. Mike was next, he was sent to a football player's home. He had watched several football tapes with the man and his teammates, even his newly wedded wife. After everyone left, Mike was forced to have sex with the woman, the footballer watched and told him what to do to his wife. As she was explored, and all her holes opened by Mike, he ate and drank alcohol like he was watching a porn movie. She was made to give Mike oral pleasure as he had to devour her simultaneously. He was so afraid that he may be killed he had a hard time completing the task. Just when he thought the deed was done, he was made to bend over and take the football player's member inside of him, he screamed out repeatedly. The wife was on her hand and knees playing with the football player's genitals as he took Mike over and over with so much force, when he dove into him, he would fall down onto his knees only to be forced back up by the football player, pulling him back into position again. The marriage was only for show, so the couple hired outside their marriage to please each other instead of having affairs to keep the secrets a secret. Deleon's first experience was also horrible. He was assigned to a priest to help with errands around the church grounds. Deleon was not aware of what was about to happen to him after these chores were done. He had just finished calling the Bingo numbers when he was directed to go down to the basement of the church. Once there two women dressed in all black with their hair covered led him into a room. He was holding a box when he was told to put the box down and lay on the bed in the room. He laid down, and just as he was about to ask what is going on? A man walked in with a robe that had something attached that looked like chains, just as he tried to raise up off the bed he was struck in the face with the robe. He was so shocked that he tried to grab his face, but he was jumped on by the two ladies and held down on the bed. The man stood over him as he was forced to put his shaft in his mouth and the women spoke words over him. He was unsure if it was a prayer or a spell, but he knew it was not right. As he threw up in his mouth from the man's member being forced into it, he cried. Once the man was finished, he was made to have anal sex with both women and lick on their private parts until they relieved themselves in his mouth. He was made to have anal sex with the man as well; this went on all night until he passed out. When he woke up, he had various markings on his body and bruises that resemble beads and symbols. All the boys were returned back to their captor. The next day they could only look at each other in terror, the words or stories of that night were never revealed but a bond was made. The boys took a vow that night to get away from that place. That was the last time the boys were separated without knowing of each other whereabouts. As the remainder of the crew tore up the streets of New York searching for their friends, these thoughts weighed heavily on both of them. They had vowed many years ago to get away and now they were making another vow to kill any and all involved with the kidnapping of their family.

CHAPTER 19

No ransom note had been received, no phone calls with any threats had been made, so the crew knew this was on a personal level. As Peter lay on the hard floor with blood covering his body, he could feel at least two of his ribs broken, he was having difficulty breathing. After he was kidnapped, he was held in a cement room with no air or heat. Peter knew when it was day or night because the weather would change, and he could feel the difference in the climate from the concrete. He was made to drink water, but no food was given in all the days since he had arrived. No one spoke to him, but he could feel that he was being watched all the time. No one was in the room he was in but the feeling of being watched or hunted all day was a given. The only sound he heard was a drip of water somewhere in the distance of the room. He slept most of the time because of the injuries he had sustained. Peter would have both good and bad dreams. He would desperately try to remember good times with Deja so that he could at least sleep a few hours out of the time there. On this day he was awakened by a bucket of something hot being thrown on him, he jumped up and realized it was blood, who's there? Peter screamed out. But no one answered, after he called several more times he was told; I thought you would like to have something from your little girlfriend! That voice was very familiar Peter thought. Oh no he thought, it can't be. Her blood is now on your hands. The mistress said, "I told you everything you liked or love would be taken from you if you disobeyed me". It took me years to find you, and now I have you, you will suffer for your disobedience. Peter tried to keep his composure but after a couple of minutes in silence, he said, If this is true, I will torture you in ways you never knew was possible, I'm going to fuck you up, he said it in almost a whisper, but she heard him and replied, so the student wants to be a teacher? Let's just see, let the games begin. From that day, Peter was fed the same scraps he would get as a child under her care. He would only eat enough not to starve, but to try to get some nutrients to heal. He could not do any exercise due to his ribs being broken but he strengthened his mind daily by meditating. When he heard someone coming, he would start counting their footsteps, when he heard any voices, he would memorize them. In the weeks that passed, he was made to stay in the room with rotting body parts that he was told were Deja's, some were so bruised or decomposed that he couldn't make out what the part was. He tried to not smell the stink, but it could not be avoided. He was chained up, so his movements were limited to say the least. He started seeing things and talking to himself. He was losing his mind. With the body parts being scattered around the room he had created a place deep within his mind for peace. The mistress was happy to see him breaking. This was all a part of her plan.

CHAPTER 20

Mike and Deleon had no leads to the whereabouts of Peter and Deja. But they both took weeks to get Russell and De'Ann back in working order. They had ordered various parts as well as made what they couldn't order. They were running tests when they remembered that both robots Russell and De'Ann had a chip in them in case they were stolen. The chips were embedded next to each of their ribcages, something each of the crew had also installed in each other for these kinds of issues. As well as being able to access each other's homes and bank accounts. In case any of them was in any trouble and couldn't access money or be found. No credit card or keys would be needed if they had to get away with nothing. After Russell and Deann's systems updated, more weapons and tactical software were added to both. They started working on tracking Peter, his whereabouts would be revealed soon, and the chaos and mayhem would be epically unleashed. Afghanistan here we come. This will be war.